No Need to Walk in a Straight Line

poems by

Dana Yost

Finishing Line Press
Georgetown, Kentucky

No Need to Walk
in a Straight Line

Copyright © 2025 by Dana Yost
ISBN 979-8-89990-101-0 First Edition
All rights reserved under International and Pan-American Copyright Conventions. No part of this book may be reproduced in any manner whatsoever without written permission from the publisher, except in the case of brief quotations embodied in critical articles and reviews.

Publisher: Leah Huete de Maines
Editor: Christen Kincaid
Cover Art and Design: Dana Yost
Author Photo: Rae J. Yost

Order online: www.finishinglinepress.com
also available on amazon.com

Author inquiries and mail orders:
Finishing Line Press
PO Box 1626
Georgetown, Kentucky 40324
USA

Contents

My Super Power 1

Escapes 3

For Sara 4

Last Pennies 6

Seduction Confession 7

The Three Bridges Trail 9

Small Noise 10

Hands 11

Prairie Storm 13

When Lilacs Bloom 14

Newspaper Days 16

The Lonely Stalk Their Front-Room Windows at Night 18

Twenty to Thirty Years 19

Our Drought 20

Flurry of Wing and Talon 23

Once Was Home 24

What A Good Walk Does 25

Human Desire 26

Obsession 27

Crows Overhead 29

Behind A Grove 30

A Shrine 32

Dusk At The Beach 34

Cedar Swing 35

In The Beauty of All This 36

Voodoo Blue 37

Freeze Out 38

Fireball 41

Another Night	42
Night Light for the Harvest	43
The River Still	44
The Land Out Here	45
Variations on Isolation	46
Bird on a Post	50
Rainbow	51
Euthanized	52
Teen-Age Days	53
Refugees: To Go On Living	54
Hoops By Myself	55
Free-Fall	57
Wedding Photo	59
Lavender	60
What Holds You	62
In With Dragonflies	63
11:43	64
Pontoon Dream	65
Sundays	66
Blue Flannel	67

In memory of Greg Riekens and Joseph Amato

My Super Power

You're looking for beauty to take the place
of those who are not here,
so someone tells me, and I believe her,
because life goes forward even when
those we want around us are elsewhere.
Do you want a super power, she asks.
What would you do with your super power?
*Beam my friends to my side, just for an hour,
so we could talk, laugh, hug.*
That's a nice super power, a strong super power,
she says. And I feel good that she thinks that way.
Of course, it's hypothetical. Even more than that,
it's dream-wishing, fool's game, no matter the warmth
it gives me.
For people's lives go on without me. They make
their own homes, fall in love, raise children,
spend too many hours at work—all the things
I wish they'd give up to be close to me.

So what do I do to replace them, those I've
lost either to death or to the continuity of life,
to moving away from those who matter?
I must look for beauty, she says, in new places,
in new hearts. It's no search for the weak,
I say, and this is so. The world is cold, is turned inward,
and to crack it you need a will as strong as an ice pick,
forever chipping. You join new committees, stand in line
for concerts, eat ice cream at the town fair. Yet, you don't
always get honest answers, or things are brought up
around you, but not to you—those new ones you want
close to you only elude you, slide up, then around,
and it's not the same. Not the same as before,
not the same as beauty.

So you continue the search.
Beauty exists in the world, you're sure of this,
the kind you're looking for. The kind you once had,
the kind you felt in the longing hold of a friend
before you said goodbye for what may be the last time.

Beauty exists in the world. If not where you've been looking,
then someplace else. When you've fallen, your hands
have not buckled, but grown stronger.
Continue the search, she says. You won't find
beauty by sitting still, but by climbing the rock,
circling the tree, waiting in line for the art show to open,
photos on canvas, a wasteland turned into grace
by the way the lens settles on leaves in a pathway.

Escapes

I listen to Mellencamp on a chilly evening,
waiting for baseball to start. Two escapes
on a day when I am reminded of divisions
in our country, on a day when an in-law
dies—either of old age or COVID, maybe both.

I need the escapes. I need walks in the woods,
looking through trees for a hint of a white tail,
maybe the flash of a fox. Always, the squirrels
with their rustle in the forest bottom. Always
think of sorrow when I listen to this Mellencamp

album: From late in his career, it's aching,
melancholy, full of regrets and misjudgments.
Whose life isn't, I suppose. But he writes
and sings it so well it brings these matters
to the surface for me. Before this, I listened

to the sermon of a friend of mine in Iowa,
thanks to the Internet. It was convicting.
Who are we to be haughty, to discriminate,
to leave the poor to fend for themselves?
On this chilly evening, I think about this, too,

as I listen to Mellencamp, as I wait for baseball.
I need to escape, but maybe I shouldn't.
Maybe there is one more thing I can do
today to help another, maybe there is
one more thing we all can do before

we snug up for the night.

For Sara

suddenly,
she's bleeding,
down her leg,
but she thinks,
this isn't me,
not me, bleeding,
but it is her, the blood has reached
her ankle, then her toes
and is running on the bathroom
tile, but she still thinks it is not
her, she wouldn't do this,
she's been in trouble
before, but never has
she done this, then her mother
is taking her to the ER,
where she gives her name,
only it doesn't feel like her name,
but someone else's,
someone she knew once
when she was a child,
when she was safe,
and the nurse looks
at her, says we'll
have you stitched
up fast, and she thinks,
it was that deep a cut?
And it was, made by her,
they say. They, including
her mother.
The stitching up will be
minor compared to what
comes next: two days, at least,
locked down in a BHU,
and all the assessments
and talking it through
and she still swears it wasn't
her, and now she hears talk
of a long-term commitment
to an intense treatment center

and she's so tired all she wants
is sleep and she sleeps on the concrete
floor that leads to the concrete wall
that holds up the sparse bunk
in her room and she sleeps on that bunk, too,
sleeps until her mother comes to visit,
to tell her we have options,
and she says this isn't me,
isn't me, and if she could only
be let go to find herself, the real
her, who is out there somewhere,
twirling her hair and running bare feet
through sand on a beach, that girl
who has gotten away from her,
if she could find her maybe
all this could go away.

Last Pennies

We should throw our last pennies
into Amtrak tickets to the Northwest
as far as we can pay for,
wherever that is, and make new lives
and live in our own humor and dreams
and when you get old and scared
I will hold you and tell you stories
about people we don't know
who all died after happy endings
to lives we didn't live,
and tell you we had a happy ending,
too, in a happy life,
this new life built far from ghosts
and gossip, a life built for two,
like a tandem bike, with comfortable seats
and an easy glide.
The moon will belong to us,
and the elk and the hawk,
and the horned owls in trees
will be in another life,
where the river is someone else's
but we won't mind, as we
slip into dreams under a blanket
borrowed from your grandmother,
flavored with the sadness of Chinese poets
who watched dynasties end
with ships sailing to the East,
while they, exiled and impoverished,
made homes in perches of hard rock
above the stream.

Seduction Confession

The Texas poet with dark hair
long and coiled, almost out-of-the-shower shine,
like an Italian morning dream
tells us she is a Christian,
"but not a very good one."
At first, I think she says this simply
for the laugh,
then she begins to read
and we see the sins swell
in her eyes, arouse moisture
on her lips with each pass of a tongue
so enjoying
the telling
of the intertwined
delights of sex and wine
long hours wrapped in sheets
of fine cloth,
of stealing touches
under banquet tables.
She has beautiful eyes,
spell-maker eyes,
a voice scruffed a bit by the cool Iowa autumn,
and this only makes the men in their metal
folding chairs love to be read to even more.

And it deceives us, such a voice, echoed as it is
by the slow swoops and touching of her chest bones
by elegant fingers,
for I slowly see
she is not seducing
but confessing
and each moment of lace and caress,
curves in late-night shadow,
is told not for us, but brought to a table
where a slender, white stole is draped
over a silver cross, and wine drips from the
side of a chalice,
the Texas poet wet at her eyes
a plea to be cleansed

again
because another night falls
and a man has found
a flower for her
which she holds as he touches her hair
as in an Italian dream.

The Three Bridges Trail

There are walks I will want to take
in my last days, and one will be the Three Bridges Trail.
Find someone to lead me, if I am frail, through
the narrow path, across the three stone bridges.
But I will see, hear, smell for myself.
It is almost primeval, the brush to my knees, even
my chest: the thick leaves turning day to night
almost as soon as we set foot on the dust and gravel.
It is like stepping beyond the curtain, into the Emerald City.
The birds flutter and sing and one says "pur-dee, pur-dee, pur-dee,"
in a branch over my head.
At other times, a stillness: no animals, the wind cut off
by the thickness of leaves: it is almost German forest, medieval.
Over there, the clearing: can't you picture a dozen furied
swords and axes clanging and cleaving, unmerciless battle?
No?
But, then, my imagination runs beyond reach of the reins.

Walk with me, in the green and the cool.
Walk with me, on the ledge of the stone
of the bridges:
the fall is not far, if it comes to that,
and the undergrowth will catch you,
soft. Blanket of a crib.
Walk with me, when those last few days are near,
and think with me not of what life might have been,
but what it was—what it is: as real as the doe
in deep staredown with us, as real as the aroma of juniper.
Did we matter? Did we lift the lives of others?
Did we love, did we give enough time to the stars,
did we dream—or was it all mad?
Look at the butterflies, the gem-green beetle.
I will walk here again, in my last days,
the Three Bridges Trail:
whatever deeds define my life,
I know finding this place
is one of the good.

Small Noise

In the woods and along the rivers
of this new place,
I find a healing and a retreat.
It is not the same as the lonely and ragged
wetland ponds of home, isolated
and at the dead ends of gravel roads,
where I could kneel and shout and weep
and know that only God and a few red-wing blackbirds
might hear.
Here, another's feet might emerge from the trees
or from around a curve in the trail,
maybe lovers embracing on a bench
beneath walnut and red oak,
or there may be a bow hunter
in camo, back against a stump,
who has to pack and haul his gear because I have come along.
But I am learning places
where there is stillness,
and distance,
that I can almost call my own.
I found a field, sloping away from a horse path
and go there to rest, amid cocklebur, saplings and wild grass,
listening to the small noises of the woods.
I become a small noise myself,
whispering prayers for relief,
worn and lonely in a worn and lonely place.

Hands

Hands and fingers: rough, scabbed,
calloused, bent, thick,
hands and fingers that do the rugged work
of turning politicians' sweetly-spun
words into the things we tell ourselves we need:
bigger homes, wider roads, faster Internet,
the red-brick/tall-windowed monuments
to ego and legacy.
It is the work of the rough,
the work of sweat,
the work of danger, caught
in a trench in the cold-water gush
of a broken pipe, waist deep, rising.
It is the work of cuffing aside
the shit of others,
of the heave and haw
of the backhoe claw,
and the hands needed to
twist, shove levers and gears,
to crank loose a decades-rusted nut,
to yank free grain from a feedmill auger,
strong hands, thick fingers.
It all says tough.

Yet, it's the forearm that says tough
in ways I still cannot bear:
Back twenty years, in his Army sergeant days,
after the Yellowstone fires,
after the Nevada desert survival training:
simply in a machine shop
at Fort Riley, outside Junction City, Kansas.
Welding a motor mount back in place,
protected by face-shielded helmet, welder's heat-retardant coat,
but not seeing a gap between glove and sleeve:
three bullets of runaway slag—molten junk metal—
find that gap, bounce and sear down the inside of the sleeve,
melting flesh on the lower side of the forearm.
I want to say shit when I hear the story,
but he's past the pain by then,

home on leave,
slowly rolling up the sleeve
to show the scars: craters of dead flesh,
gray and pocked, like an old man's mouth.

I've shaken the hands,
been bear-hugged by the arms:
he could crush bone if it came to it,
I think.
But I've also seen him bent over a pool table,
limbo-leaning under the bar lamp,
the cue a cellist's bow in those hands,
master's tap bringing forth a note
that spins the cue ball and, like the touch of a new father,
taps the striped 12-ball into a side pocket,
cue ball knowingly stopping,
sweetly aligned for the next shot,
the one that means the trophy and cash
from the big tournament in Sioux Falls,
the title for which there is only one winner,
the one whose hands and fingers
leave shadows over the green felt
but never a scratch.

Prairie Storm

The bruised half-hour after a prairie storm,
layers of sickly white, sun-starved cloud
and ill, disoriented, gray-whale sky
overlap and hang, the storm a dumbfounded thing
droning away to the east. There are no
mountain-sized thunderheads in a storm like this,
just a slow thickness that means rain and relief to brittle farmland,
perhaps some vicious downdrafts that strip and twist a grove of maple,
but nothing that lands you in the news.
And be grateful for that.

The news comes for the dead, the shredded, the sobbing,
the images that can't be explained by science or God:
half a house in splinters, but the baby's bedroom left perfect and pink;
necktie rack blown forty miles, ten ties still attached, clean;
farmyard mud driven through the pores of the century-old farmhouse's walls,
the house still standing and solid, but the interior looking as if painted in
dirt, every wall, every floor, every threshold, even the bathtub,
and the wife on the front steps, wordless
and her palms as muddy as if she'd been swimming in earth, silently
permitting entrance to seemingly every oddity-seeker in Minnesota.
The storm today performs none of that.
It is business-like and plodding, and the bruises will heal,
and that is enough
to keep the prairie living, blossoming for a few more weeks.

When Lilacs Bloom

The neighbor's lilacs in thick
bloom, lavender and lush.
A thrush, startled
by mid-morning door-slam, darts
to refuge between blossom and branch.
I am reminded of Whitman's
tribute to the dead Lincoln.
A pair who saw the world
not as a line to be stood upon
one side or the other,
but as a freshly born sphere—every slight turn
a bending lead to new arrays,
sunlight leaving shadow
neither black nor white
but an infinite arc of gradients—azure blue
to buttercup to Tuscan red.
Minds self-trained to absorb
thought the way their eyes
took in color, each,
if seeded in a meadow, sprouting
another stem, blade, leaf
that springs in shouting vibrancy
from the sphere.

Have I taken you a long way from lilacs?
I don't think so:

behind the lilacs,
our neighbor's tall ash
is luscious green and our red maple
a waxen
maroon, and, beneath,
grass green, yellow,
brown, and an intersection of city streets: faded-to-gray
asphalt, dirty-white curb and gutter.
See the world in all its colors.
Not just with your eyes,
but with all that pulses

in you.
When lilacs bloom,
bloom with them.

Newspaper Days

I slept too long

                                again

dreaming of my newspaper days

not of the long hours but of closing

a story—the finishing touches

on something that might shed light

on a scandal in a small town,

the mayor's wrongdoing

malfeasance by the city manager

papers given to us under

                                the door
the quiet frenzy

or maybe an opinion column

where I came to the defense

                                of immigrants

something that would shake our readers

at any rate

but it wasn't true.   not any more

because it was a dream and I haven't

worked in newspapers for a dozen years

lost the ability, the outlet, to make an

                              impact

maybe I still could but more likely I cannot

it's what they call aging, changing careers

leaving behind hard work in a hurting industry,

leaving it to others, yet still suffering

with sympathy, even grief, for what I once

had, and no longer   do

The Lonely Stalk Their Front-Room Windows at Night

The lonely stalk their front-room windows at night,
watching snowflakes fall
in streetlight shadows, silent,
a robe over their shoulders,
rolling prayers and pleas through the folds of their minds,
standing until weary legs say "please." Eventually
day, night, light, dark
become the same, days are lost, holidays missed,
the front-room window a smear of old dreams,
vanished conversation.
Feral cats slash by,
indifferent
to the fingertip tap on the glass,
pausing only to piss yellow
into the cold white snow.

Twenty to Thirty Years

Twenty to thirty years—
was it really that long?
Not really, she thought, at last.
Surely, if she had lasted forty-five years,
she could last another twenty to thirty
and, convinced now of this fact,
she slipped the rope off from her throat.

She went outside to sit at her patio table,
and the geraniums were growing tall and full
and she allowed their petals to tickle her calves.
Then came the honeybees, and wasps which circled
around her head, then circled around her face.
How interminable.

Her friend brought over lunch, sandwiches
on a plate wrapped with cellophane. They talked
about gardens, gossiped about people they had in common,
and wondered about the weather. In passing,
she said the love of her life had upped and moved away
without so much as a goodbye or leaving a forwarding address.
Of course, she had never told him he was the love of her life,
she had only daydreamed it—for years—and then he was gone
before she could ever say it. How she lamented it.

They continued talking about gardens and the weather,
the friend not acknowledging what she had said about the love
of her life, glossing over it as she spoke of aster and violets.
Then, would it rain tonight, or tomorrow night?
How banal it seemed, it all seemed.
How banal it would seem for the next twenty to thirty years.

Our Drought

I.
At a state wetland south of us called Eagle Lake,
there is no lake this summer. Not even marsh
or sickly green bog. Everything has dried,
exposing hollow logs
obviating the warning of the
official sign at the public access: "No aquatic hitchhikers."
It means don't transport toxic
weeds from one lake
to another with your boat.
No problem: if there's no aqua,
there's no aquatic hitchhikers.

II.
This is a hard drought. Only the foolish
light a grill, only the greedy
turn on a lawn sprinkler.
But yesterday, the heat broke, and the town
flexed like a big cat finally
freed from a cage. No rain, but no stifled air.
Relief.
What I saw:
One of the girls next door lets her dog out at noon,
and sits with him on the brown
lawn. "Finally," she tells me,
"I can breathe."
Neighbors fuss with the scraps of their gardens,
the Vietnamese woman's white baseball cap
bobbing like a distant sail as she bends,
rises, bends, hoe in hands,
cleaving away dried earth, the rot
of failed plants. In the town-square
gazebo, a woman sits reading
from her Kindle, stroking the nape
of a black poodle on her lap.
On the paved path along the shriveled river,
a man parks his Jeep, reads
the newspaper with his door open,
left leg

dangling
    on the runner,
his twelve-year-old
Irish setter
dozing in the gravel
near the front wheel.
There is the rattle and rumble of delivery trucks
being unloaded: hand carts hurried
down metal ramps
on the hill
of a downtown street. A high-schooler
on a red motorcycle
shimmies between two trucks, a moment
like a European city, a scene
from a *Bourne* movie.

III.

I shiver in my white T-shirt on my morning walk,
but there is no complaining: for too many days,
I was wiping sweat
from the back of my neck
before I opened the door.
Is it climate change? A rebirth
of the Dust Bowl Thirties?
I have theories, but for now, I am content thinking
about the dogs and gardens and the armada
of clouds which stretches
beyond the limits of sight,
am content listening to the playful screams
of neighbor boys as they chase one another
in a game of tag, as the clocks
turn toward noon.

IV.

We are the inverse of those who dwell
inside the Arctic Circle, those pent
up for months of darkness and skin-blackening cold.
We have been imprisoned
by three months of record heat,

half-naked in our living rooms, central air
gushing sweet
deception toward our eyes and chests.
I think we all want to join the little neighbor boys
in their screams: therapeutic
ecstasy: Good God, this is
good.
Let it last.

V.
South of here, they are already chopping corn for silage,
and farther south, in Missouri,
digging wells in a desperate flurry.
Eagle Lake is not the only thing gone dry.
On the TV news, a woman
rancher is watching her cattle die.

Flurry of Wing and Talon

On a gravel road in Lincoln County,
scouting hunting sites,
my brother, my young
nephew, me,
side-by-side-by-side on the pickup's
bench seat,
scrolling past
     groves,
          fields,
               old farmsteads.
A blue-sky afternoon.
My nephew
goes *"whoa,"*
gets us to turn
our heads in time
to see a wide-winged bird—an owl or a hawk—
scoop a gopher out of field stubble.
Death, in a flurry
of wing and talon,
and we remember
the prairie
is a harsh place,
and not everything
survives.

Once Was Home

A near-buried farmhouse,
heaved and collapsed,
husk,
swallowed by vines
that have swollen to python size.
Raccoons in the upstairs now,
and old chemical barrels in the shed.
This used to be my home,
an old man says.
He tells us about breakfast smells
and sleeping three boys to a bed
in a family of thirteen children.
The front door is gone,
whether ripped away or given to the pecking microbes of decay,
we can't say: not even a board from the frame
to lean on.
The old man lifts his cap:
thinning hair, scalp red and brown from years
of hardy farm work.
He waves his cap, whether as a farewell
or in frustration, we can't say,
but it is upside down in his hand,
and if it were to rain, would quickly fill.
But it is a dry summer, and there's no risk.
A gust through the grove, and there's a touch
of human voice to it:
of the past,
of heaven,
of the dead,
we can't say.
It is a dry summer
and a fire could easily burn.

What a Good Walk Does

In my youth, I never liked
walking farm fields: the dirty-socked, sweaty
work of pulling
weeds, picking
rock, with the hope
of a plastic cup of juice at the end of a long row.

Now, I lace heavy boots, and thump
the dirt field roads with purpose and pleasure:
smell the fresh-cut hay,
the sweat of cattle;
breathe in the blue sky.
To doctors, I want to say: prescribe
this for everyone in the room,
the hunched-over
hyperventilators; the timid, talking to the walls;
the small wife, perpetually
sad; the blade survivors;
send them into the open fields,
give them a good lunch,
a bird guide book,
and explain
there's no need
to walk in a straight line.

Human Desire

I like movies,
but make them good,
make them real,
as real as the soul
in pain, say like *Human Desire*,
the classic with Glenn Ford
and that great Gloria Grahame,
where every moment aches
so much you almost can't bear it,
where love is raw, at bone level,
and cutting into it is like death
itself, unless you're so good
at faking it it still seems real,
still hurts, still opens the human soul
like a knife through warm flesh
—give me that in a movie
and I'll sit for two hours
nonstop watching it,
waiting for the killer to break apart,
for the cold-hearted—or is she?—woman
to end up dead on the floor of a moving
train, for love at its purest to prevail,
raw, as simple as a day after war,
fishing or at a dance, as simple
as that, as that.

Obsession

I turn myself inside out,
as if pulling my flesh outward,
but really my mind—
pulling it to the surface
to find out what's obstructing
it, what it is I keep thinking
about to the near-exclusion
of all else.
I examine my thoughts,
my recesses. I share them
with my therapist week
after week. Like a fog
settled over me,
or the return of low-grade depression,
or some kind of actual thought,
an obsession,
that's jammed in my mind
like a stick between the spokes
of a child's bike.

After a time, I decide I may know,
may have a clue,
but am afraid to pursue it,
for what it might say about me,
about my life and those in it.
Too dangerous, too damaging,
too damned tempting,
a thing dangling before
my mind like juice dripping
from a bottle, tempting
with its tastes and touches.
So I work on ways to turn myself
back inside, bring the thing
to a quieter, more remote place
where it won't steal at me
so much, won't say "come to me,"
with all the implications those words
hold. I work on burying them,
busying myself with other thoughts,

with life in the real world, tangible,
like polishing the wood on the dining room
table, like walking in the heat, breathing
in the warm air and sifting my breath
for aromas from the houses I pass:
lilacs or baking bread or the sweat
of a dog just finished with a walk.

I read about foreign people,
I read about history,
I twist at night in my bed, working
to think of tomorrow, not that thing
that tempts. I sleep and dream
of old work days, and wake to
new tasks, new words—cicerone,
for one—and drag my mind
through the hard work of another day,
where reality, whiler duller than temptation,
is better for me, safer, even cozier.

Crows Overhead

What if there is only the drift,
the broken limbs and dead leaves
falling from bare trees in the woods where I walk,
as aimless
as my next days, and ending up
in the open-water patches of the river,
slow spins toward the oblivion of mud?
I say all this aloud, walking as I do,
losing my way in the asking:
In front of me, a farm with a small, fenced-off lot
for cattle: they look up from their feed,
blank, dead-beast stares.
Open sky, away from the woods.
Crows overhead, and the cattle's breath
comes out as coughs of steam.
Someone in the Old Testament
might have said this means something,
and I might have, too, on a former day.
Crows overhead,
but their circling paths
lead them
nowhere.

Behind A Grove

A hard, hard life,
the pioneers,
sod-busters,
turning earth
one row at a time,
pulling plow by hand,
or, if they somehow squeezed
the money, behind a raggedy horse.
Winters froze cattle to death
standing up,
turned babies' skin red, then blue,
then black:
bury them after the thaw.
If diphtheria sweeps through,
takes every child,
you burn their clothes,
douse the bodies
with lye,
bury them together.
White angel. Fire angel.
Where my grandmother was born,
every building is now gone—the wood rotted,
or borrowed for another place,
the grove haggard,
and behind it, a pioneer cemetery,
half-dozen plots unmarked,
two holding the bones of children
lumped together in 1893,
others with the limestone markers
fallen, cracked, blackened,
names almost smeared smooth, illegible,
by wind, rain, time.
An Eagle Scout has been restoring it,
hammering in new fencing,
cementing in a new flag pole,
sifting death certificates to at least
list the names on a poster.
My blood down in those holes,
or some of it—my grandmother's cousins,

aunts, uncles.
I've had my photo taken near the flagpole
and a metal-pipe cross painted white.
Always in the summer, though, the photos.
Behind me, in one shot, the marker
for a woman named Mary
is prone in the prairie grass,
split horizontally. She died
at nineteen
in a winter month.

A Shrine

At Cooperstown, my family
gave me a day to myself
to spend time in the gallery,
to walk slowly through the exhibits,
to marvel at Rogers Hornsby's bat,
Lou Gehrig's locker—broken down,
removed from Yankee Stadium, reassembled—
Rod Carew's jersey. So many ghosts,
so much history. All the things I dream
of when I am alone in my room,
and now, here before me. This
place is a treasure, and I am not
the only one who believes this, of course.
The streets are coated with tourists,
some just curious visitors, some
as serious about it as I am.
And this is not even Induction Weekend.
Just a mid-week day in June.
Yet, the throngs.
I stand in front of a life-size carving
of Ted Williams and admire the left-handed swing.
I kneel to see baseballs signed by pitchers
who threw no-hitters.
I wonder how much concentration it took
to hit with the greatness of Ty Cobb.
I wonder how much more concentration it took
to play at Jackie Robinson's level, batting
.342 in 1949 despite the hatred, the bigotry
of sections of the crowd, the invectives flung
in his face, in letters to his home.
I retrace my steps, end up in the gallery,
where the plaques of the greats hang,
where Harmon Killebrew and Ralph Kiner
and Christy Mathewson are immortalized
—as long as this place exists, they
will be remembered.
Finally, I walk out, elevated, justified
in my obsessions, the day still golden,
off to the north the sun shining

on Lake Otsego, baseball
as close a thing to a god as we have
in this life.

Dusk at the Beach

But then comes night,
the onset of beauty
and calm, sunset
dripping reds and yellows
through the trees, clouds,
until they reflect upon the blue, yellow, gold ripplets
of the water,
and the darkening greens of shoreline
trees—a blender of color and mood
that always pours out perfectly
into the glass upon the picnic table,
the one I drink from when I am lonely,
sad, and need to know
the world still works wonders
upon our souls.

Cedar Swing

A cedar swing in the back yard,
gliding over September grass.
Fireflies twirl and circle us,
a serenade in dance.
This is what you like,
a small bonfire's orange warmth
and the smell of apple wood,
kittens licking and tickling our bare toes,
the grove a dusky silhouette of shelter
to our west.
We are comfortable here,
or is that a strong enough word?
Content, happy, cozy—
in love, I'd say,

but why not this:
a wordless sway,
adults in the bliss
of childhood dream,
holding hands,
moony-eyed,
long after
the blurring butterscotch
of sunset
has yielded
to shadow
and starlight.

In the Beauty of All This

Out here, we are tourists starting a search for Mount Hood,
two hundred miles away, and big, of course,
snow-topped and big. But so many are,
so many snow tops on the wide circle of horizon.
We pull our rental car to the shoulder at an intersection,
and it's no longer the mountain I need to find
but something larger, something more
than even the vast dry spaces of eastern Oregon:
my place in this world again,
my one slot in the beauty of the whole thing,
which I've misplaced like my keys,
but I need right now.
Here, I remember the beauty of places
and remember the beauty of people.
We hold hands and pull close, and though I can see snow-topped
mountains they seem very small.
I have a place in the beauty of all this,
and I know where it is.

Voodoo Blue

Cross your heart and try
not to bleed. This is not
a prayer.
Eat a bone, pet the dog.
Remember? Her name was
Trixie her name was. She was
your grandfather's
and they buried her
in the hole within the grove.
Nose wet and cold,
        how she lapped
at the silver-tin water bucket,
thin tail wagging like a bone
in a voodoo woman's paw.
I don't want to live in the past,
but the past wants to live in me.

Here's a field stone: black, streaked
with chalk-like white, weight
of an anvil. Heave it upon your back.
It says:
turn cold against the world
if you want
to survive it.

Freeze Out

My son wants us to walk
to the middle of Lake Calhoun today.
Thirteen below overnight
and the ice is a thick reflector
of the Minnesota morning.
It's beautiful, he says.
And it is:
a mirror that captures sun dogs
that look as if they've passed through
stained glass,
the gliding clouds
like white cloth.
A symmetry in the semi-circle
of bare trees that enfold
the far shore.
Christmas comes in four days,
and this has the look of tinsel
and Tiffany, a serenity
borrowed from painters who show
us the nostalgic, pastoral glow
of Christmases
that never were,
but are what we wanted
them to be.

My son wants to stand
in the center,
arms wide,
part of the symmetry.
I get it: it's like
inserting yourself
into a painting
—the almost-sacred
winter silence.
He points: the sun striking
the lake, making
a pink halo
on the sheen.
Come on, he says.

But I am afraid
of ice,
even if eighteen inches thick.
I've written news stories about people
drowning
when they fell
through holes
in lake ice.
My uncle
went under
on a river, sliding
along with the current
until someone punched
a hole and pulled him out.
When I have
been on lake ice,
I've winced
at each creak,
each groan,
waiting for the cataclysmic
split.

There are other people
out there, my son says. They
look like they're having fun.
I insist: *no*. And I know
my fear disappoints him.
I say: won't it be just
as pretty, just as wondrous
if we stand by that bench
on shore, and look
out at the lake?
It won't, of course.
The symmetry
is off. The sun reflects
differently. The bench
is too close to a busy Lake Street,
and, thus, too loud.
Where's that sacred silence?

It won't be the same.
He knows it.
I know it.
We say no more,
and walk away,
my son wanting
to be somewhere
I could not
take him.

Fireball

Late now,
a night of working out grief
in poetry scratched a line
at a time on torn-thin
paper scraps and pilfered
memo pad. I say a few prayers.
But I will not sleep.
I'm broken somehow,
like a papier-mâché creature fallen
from shelf. There's no
prayer for that, I think.
Small glass of wine,
streak of orange-yellow light
in the sky. I'll stay up.
Maybe the fireball made it to earth.
Maybe I could find it.
Maybe I could measure the scar.

Another Night

Another night waking.
Another night the sweats.
Another night walking to the railroad bridge.
The choir of crickets and tree frogs,
an owl in the trees, something
my half-Lakota friend would call an omen.
Beneath, the river holds the gray reflection
of the moon, its face as tired as my own.

Another night worn.
Another night television's political clatter
from the street's open windows:
the seething angry, the gloating belligerent,
forever on the precipice of a shove.
But strength, as the song goes, is not the same as violence.

Another night saying I want to be strong.
Saying I want the strength in the mercy and forgiveness of the meek,
in the patience of the dispossessed,
in the hope of the beaten-down,
in how I used to be:
calm in a sandstorm, saying this passes
and I'll hold your hand until it does.

What I want is the strength
of the stone slipping without sound
into the river beneath,
in its ripples a constancy, a force
that reaches the banks, spreads downriver
through bends, cuts and bows
to places I have never been.
In its ripples, a constancy
that harnesses my frenetic heartbeat.
Within that stone's fall,
the strength to reach, within and without, beyond what can be seen.

Night Light for the Harvest

Sickle-shaped moon,
polished,
as if its edges
had been whetted
                                    and it had cut
what it had been asked to cut
then wiped clean
                                    and hung in the sky
like a tool on a workshop wall.

The River Still

The river still
this Sunday morning,
a place to lie down,
the current's slow spill like
a mother's calming stroke
upon the back of the neck.
The native grass and cat tails,
the tiny voices of house wrens and warblers
like a backup choir, distant,
but integral—
in place to smooth disruptions
back to placid.

I count fishing boats tied
on the far shore, and
remember mornings
casting for rough fish with my grandfather
and my brothers.
I lean over the water
and spy a sluggish bullhead, its gray shape shadow-boxing
with a gleaming stone:
a jab, a hook, then, swoosh, it darts into shadow.

The Land Out Here

When I walk the land out here,
I hear crying: words of too-late warning,
then mothers for sons,
fathers for daughters, husbands
for wives.

When I walk the land out here,
I feel the cut of blade
into bone.
Cold, then hot like a scream
that shakes my ribs.

When I walk the land out here,
I think of cheating.
Word broken, paper worthless,
the thundering hooves
a nightmare of lied-over ink.

When I walk the land out here,
I see Blood Run, village
for 8,500 years, larger than any town
I have lived in. I say study it: learn
why it lasted, then why it did not.

Variations on Isolation

"Pour over me. Pour over me. Let your rain flood this thirsty soul."
   —Stuart Townend

"I see the words on a rocking horse of time. I see birds in the rain."
   —Pearl Jam

I. Night
In bed, but unasleep,
watching the red display
of the clock like a bug.
1:16 becomes 1:17.
I gather two pillows,
head to the living room floor,
and sleep face down,
gilded by the reflected gleam
of lush frost on the trees outside:
clean and lavishly white like jewelry of the rich,
a woman, perhaps, wearing it on bare throat,
long wrist, to a party where she's meeting
a man.

II. Speck
Billions of stars,
billions of galaxies.
We look up, a speck, an erasable bit
of pencil scratch.
Some say this makes us tiny, insignificant,
and they pout their way
to oblivion. I say: why not celebrate
communion with something large and alive,
where even a speck
can see another speck's twinkle across the black, noiseless sea,
and in the morning have toast and tea and dance in the sunlight
to a waltz on the radio.

III. Asteroid
In Minneapolis alone
among hundreds of thousands:
I am an asteroid amid the planets and moons and comets:

space dirt and gouged-away flanks of metal, brutishly shaped,
in a drunk-wandering spin through the place.
Yet, there is solace in this kind of solitude:
a peace without judgment, a meal without interjections.
I see a movie I want to see
—*Notorious* at the Uptown, and eat rainbow trout,
fried and lemon-seasoned.
The next day, I'm early for the ballgame,
so I linger on the outdoor concourse through
a cooling October afternoon.
I blurt the name of a Hall-of-Famer
walking past me in high-priced-and-shiny black suit
—say his name with such shameless, familiar
ease it embarrasses *him:*
does he know me from somewhere?
I'm matter-of-fact, Jack, kicking back, and I rap
a hard set of knuckles
on the painted-blue iron pipe of a stadium railing: Like that.

What is this thing that possesses us,
the desire to be alone and savor it?
To not be lonely, but free,
and to find the solitude of anonymity
in the city as comforting as a bird-watching stroll
in the woods in autumn?
I know the apogee of the loneliness orbit,
of course: to be so alone you cry for a warm hand
on your shoulder, that you linger
in a café raking in waitress gossip as if it were casino change.
Long days, days of bruised soul
and sob-chafed throat,
and I have lived them.
But I crave the perigee now:
the asteroid broken from its pack,
pin-wheeling, jagged chunk
—mere speck, yes, of the cosmic whole:
single pair of feet, not quite the bumpers and axles of I-35
—but on a free ride,
no tether, no other, no deadline.

After the ballgame, pizza from a shop
where it's home-made, and a lazy rest
on a bench at Lake Calhoun,
watching the stars, looking to see what burns.

IV. Brick
Soldiers under a stone bridge in Algeria, 1943,
bone breaking, blood streaming:
mortars have caught them against the stone,
shrapnel smacks like sluggers' flailing fists,
blades taped to the knuckles.
An alley behind a small-town ballroom, 1979,
bone breaking, blood streaming:
a seventeen-year-old boy, drunk, desperate,
punches his fists into the brick exterior
of the ballroom, wails the name of a girl
who has rejected him. Stumbles, spits, sags
into the pea-rock gravel of the alley.
It's all gone quiet: the rock
band inside is on break between sets.
He screams the girl's name again.
A braying that punctures the brick, ricochets
off black-cased speakers, beer pitchers
emptied and spun sideways on steel tables.
The girl hears, and runs to the restroom,
locking the drab-green door of the stall,
but her name chases after her, a bleating
now, puddles of failure, the boy
—hands gone white bone and graveled-up flesh
—slapping away the offers of friends trying to lift him,
blood like spittle on their faces.
Algeria, 1943: the dead begin to swell,
float off in the dirty river. There is no chaplain
to pray, and the living clutch holes in the earth,
all of life untended, names wailed, then lost,
fists into brick, the dead and the lost, a mire
the stars cannot clear.

V. Beggar
Old women doing gossip
over their clothes lines are disgusted
when they see me: a beggar
licking at dust, so starved and ragged.
They spit, and so do I,
although mine is dry, a cough of air
that hasn't the strength to land,
is hauled away by the growled breath
of a basset tethered to the clothes line post.
I can't tell you anything,
can't tell myself, either,
can't ask it, so disgusted
of the turns in my life I live among the wretches.
The old women know,
and in their foreign language
they wrap my name in profanities.
I reach for the light bulb, wanting to screw
it out of place, but the socket bobs away
from reach, and my hand lands in the hound's sloppy mouth,
and the women spit.
School children sing on a hill,
at recess among junipers and chocolate bars.
I'll never see them,
but maybe someone will bury me
in that lullaby.

•••

Harpoon, sword
and a deep breath of dust.
I am a desperate wanderer.
Rocking horse in the burn barrel, it cannot gallop home.

Bird on a Post

Blackbird
on a
post.
Car turning
left, traveling
too fast
for this
residential
street.

What if
it hits
me, I think.
Will the
blackbird
sing
the song
of my life
or will
I die
unattended?

What a
thing
to think
on a sunny
Thursday
morning.
I whistle
a tune
whose name
I don't
remember.
I walk
home,
and step
into the
shower.

Rainbow

Through the window
the sun blew into
a glass of white wine
then refracted into a rainbow
upon the skin of lemon-pepper chicken
as we talked about Nazi death camps
and soldiers killed by sniper fire
in Vietnam. A teacher dead
in the recent derecho.
It was such a peaceful
setting for death, wasn't it?
The seven of us around the table
and one finally mentioned
amnesty for draft-dodgers,
and no one went berserk,
no one even disagreed.
We shook our heads
at the insanity of war,
at the cruelty of death,
and my classmate
posted photos on Facebook
of herself in hospice,
ready to die from cancer.
"I'll be here for the end,"
she said from her living room
couch, under a blanket. I looked
for a rainbow but saw only
red and yellow
and someone shot Custer
to save his life.

Euthanized

I don't need to be anthologized.
Just euthanized
For my own damn good.
Otherwise,
I'm likely to riot,
Burn something down,
Or burn my way into your heart
Leaving only a hole
The size of a prick from a dart.

Teen-Age Days

A carton full of shoes,
none my size. A full-ton
pickup, its tailgate removed.
Balloon men and raggedy
jeans. I run to the outskirts
of town, to where dust
meets the asphalt.
I squat in the bean fields
hacking milkweed with a hoe.
Swisher Sweets in my breast pocket,
smoked at a park in the country.
Someone stole my red
bicycle, rode it up the hill.
I kissed a girl in the basement
of my parents' house.
The smell of beer on my
mother's breath.
To get away from it all,
my brother and I threw a football
in the rain across two
lawns, neither of us saying
a word, just heaving the ball
in arcs that called down
the sky.

Refugees: To Go On Living

The woman from Lutheran Social Services
sends an e-mailed update on refugees from the Ukraine.
They are many, they are in peril, and some
are starting to make their way to the United States.
They are also brave, enduring what I can only imagine
are nights of fear and uncertainty, of wondering
who to trust, who not to trust, who is going
to get them someplace safe.
A child is pictured on TV, displaced, alone,
his parents on another bus, another train,
dispossessed until some kind people give him
shelter, hope, a cell phone to call his mother.

To wear the same clothes day after day,
to eat canned food and shower maybe
once a week in shelters or old schools
—better than waiting to be shelled
or killed by Kalashnikovs, of course,
—but still a hard way to live.
I hear a poet read about other refugees,
those from Gaza, and think, too, of
those who've fled death in Africa.
They, too, are brave. They survive,
they are survivors. They are reminders
of how comfortable our lives
can be in America, how soft.
Could I withstand weeks in a refugee
camp? I doubt it. I would crumble,
curl in a corner and cry. I could not
go on. Yet, so many refugees do.
A woman in the newspaper says
she lost her home, her son,
but carries with her her daughter
and a bag of clothing. Where will
she end up? She does not know.
But she owes it to her daughter
to go on living.

Hoops By Myself

On the basketball court
in the back yard,
I am shooting from the wing.
I am Phil Chenier
from the Washington Bullets of the '70s.
Then I am Norm Van Lier
of the Chicago Bulls, driving the lane.
These ballplayers from my childhood
come to mind when I shoot
hoops by myself. Maybe it is this
way for anyone.
A dog trots past, pulling its
owner by the leash: a St. Bernard,
clearly weighing more than the
50 pounds allowed by the HOA.
Should I report it?
I don't want to be the bad guy,
the snitch. I look the other way.
I shoot again but the prairie wind
carries the ball to the left, so far
it misses not only the rim
but the entire backboard
and bounds across the grass.
I fetch it and try layups
for a while to cut through the wind.
I am an isolato, to use an old word.
Me. Myself. I. Alone out here,
as I am alone inside, only
inside I have my books.
But my doctor says I need
the exercise, too. Man does not
live by words alone, she jokes.
On the basketball court,
I practice hook shots now,
like Kareem used to so
so gracefully. Mine bounce
and clank, sometimes go in,
sometimes fall off to the side.
These ghosts of the '70s

laugh at me, I think. "We'd
never miss as badly as you."
They're right. But they didn't
have to contend with the wind.
I lift a shot from the free-throw line.
It goes in with a swish. I pump
a fist. "Yes." Yes.

Free-Fall

to have no
                rules
                          no gravity

to free-fall above my mother's
Japanese garden,
above her patio table
                          where she sits
with her coffee   and menthol cigarettes

to fall back in time   to see this
my mother who is long dead
but lives strong in my mind, my heart

to have no
                rules
to travel back   more than a century
find myself in the batter's box
                against the great Walter Johnson
fireballer sidearmer
and somehow tag one   take it deep
out of the ballpark and be cheered
                             as a hero
even though it means breaking
                  Johnson's heart
since he is still looking for his first World Series
victory which will not come
              until 1924   not in my
surprise at bat against him   I don't know
how to feel about this: heroic or dream-buster
bum to let down Johnson whose picture hangs
on the side of my book shelf   who died young
of brain cancer   to free-fall to such
a dilemma

to have no
                rules
                        no laws
so when I pick a wild flower

up comes peace not just   in my heart
but for the world which is now up to me to
figure how to share   how to shake this plant
in every direction so that its seeds land
on everyone
peace for everyone
what a   dream
peace for you
this is what I pull from deep within the earth
when I tug at the wild flower
out in the woods
peace

no rules
                just that

how wonderful
even if a dream

Wedding Photo

One of my cousin's children dug it up online:
a photo and writeup
of my parents' wedding from 1959,
the photo showing my mother
at all of 18, smiling, blond,
glancing downward at the camera.
I wonder what was said
between her and the photographer,
between her and my father
on that memorable day,
between her and my grandmother,
who surely was worried about
the new hands my mother would be in.
I wonder if my mother had any
foreshadowing of what was
to come: the five children,
the eleven grandchildren,
the cancer that she fought
for eleven years then finally
stilled her heart. Even the second
marriage after my father died young.
If she'd had any foreknowledge,
would she have gone through
with it, would she have still
said yes and gone on to live
as she really did, with the good,
the hard days in front of her,
the days to be proud,
the days of difficult decisions,
the days of re-wallpapering
the big old house,
the days of sitting, worn out,
in the sun-room addition,
cigarette in one hand,
lighter in the other,
a deep breath,
then the inhalation
of menthol.

Lavender

In a marshy field,
park management
mowed down rows
of sumac, leaving
the hard roots exposed,
waiting to die.
It was a way to clear
off unwanted bush,
I suppose, and a reminder
that not everyone
likes everything that grows
—some see a nuisance,
some see something
unpretty that they are
content to let wither,
then fade away.
Life is like that, too,
and I feel a thud
in my heart as I stand
over the field,
a loss, an emptiness.
Later, we travel
to the Loess Hills
where someone
is growing lavender,
turning its oil
into soap, handkerchiefs,
wall art, cooking spice.
A reminder that the prairie
gives life, often in abundance,
and my heart rebounds.
I buy a kerchief, wrap
it around my neck
and inhale the fragrance.
It smells like prairie,
but more: like life itself,
and I want to lay
in the garden, butterflies
and dragonflies lighting

on my toes then blowing
where the wind takes them,
toward the hills, the sky,
toward freedom.

What Holds You

One of those days when you were sure
she was not going to live but a few hours more,
and you thought about your childhood with her,
you thought melancholy things,
you thought about her reading books
to you when you were two, three,
and the way that shaped the rest of your life,
you thought about walks in the small town
under elm trees that later died of disease,
and about how she cooked you white rice
sprinkled with cinnamon, not because it was
a delicacy but was what she could afford
on your father's meager pay.

You thought about losing her,
what memories you hadn't yet
shared with her, what stories
from her own path she hadn't yet
told you. But then she woke
from sleep and said she felt
better and she lived yet another
night and another day and things
continued on, and you still thought
the things you thought, undaunted by death,
because you knew it was coming,
would come and then it did,
and you lay there next to her,
as if waiting for another memory,
yet you felt nothing but grief
        beginning its slow, long
wend into your soul.

In With Dragonflies

How close to anger
can I come before I burst,
before I curse the infernal
stupidity, lack of care, lack of heart
of some in this nation
of ours? So selfish,
playing politics with the lives
of others, so misogynistic,
in the word of another writer,
that it leaves one longing
to spit in their faces, leaves
one longing for the power
to reroute the words of
those in power. But I am
a simple man, no office-holder,
no influencer. I take humbler
paths, the anger riding on
my shoulder like a quiet
passenger. I walk a park
trail near where I live,
inhaling the aroma of lavender,
looking for the woodpecker
on the cottonwood,
pausing to let a fawn
pass in front of me.
My anger subsides,
but not the urge to do something,
to invoke change, to make this
a better place. I lift a baby turtle
from the path, carry it to the tall
grass where it continues its
slow walk. I watch the blue
and green bodies of dragonflies
in the brush, sometimes popping
up around my face. In my anger,
I find room for wonder.

11:43

11:43 and something like sleep
is finally kicking in.
It's one of my pills,
pulling me under,
into light-sleep dreams:
a New York woman,
long and elegant,
black dress slit at the knees.
Dorothy Parker writing
about being an anti-fascist.
Me, out back, shooting
hoops on the playground
cement.
Then, darkness, but
I tumble, tear at
the bedding, I find
when I wake. It's
turmoil, twisted
and a-twirl,
wrapped around
my legs and torso.
What weighs
in my sleep
to do that?
It is not the
darkness of death,
then, but of a different
life, the unconscious,
I see that, yet nothing
tells me if I dance
with the woman
from New York.

Pontoon Dream

In my mother's house,
a photo of my father holding
a walleye in both hands.
My father grins, almost a proud boy again,
his eyes a squint under white cap.
I dreamed of this yesterday,
of my father knowing how to glide
a pontoon softly between reeds,
hover it over hungry fish,
use the right silvery lure,
and, with cigarette between lips,
give a light flick.

Sundays

There are four of us.
Nomads turned stay-at-homes.
Reunited, virtually, on Sunday mornings
by the cyber-magic of Zoom.
Chats that free us
from the mundane,
the lock-downs,
the pain of isolation.
I in my study upstairs,
the rest in their homes,
hundreds of miles of distancing.
We talk of things big
and small: Gospel commands
and governors' reticence
that borders on insolence, incompetence;
our casseroles and books we are reading, bird feeders
that draw not gold finches
but flocks of unwanted grackles.
We talk of masks and gloves
and ordering groceries online.
We talk of how we miss
what we once had, coffee-cup visits
on Sunday mornings in a small room
next to the nursery, soul-baring stuff
of four divorces, two new marriages,
near-job-loss, four moves,
depression and what Christ
would do in today's unsettled life.
We talk, virtually, of what might
change the world, and if the world
should be changed, and shrug
not with indifference but acceptance
at what we cannot change. Each week,
we start with our good mornings,
end with farewells as genuine as full-body
hugs, and I, at least, walk downstairs
with my coffee mug emptied,
but my soul refilled.

Blue Flannel

A fragment of a blue flannel shirt,
wind-frayed and snagged, hangs
in the branches of a red maple.
It's not mine—the shirt. But I pass
it each day on my walk.
So I claim it as a mental possession,
like a tick mark on a list of things
that tracks where I am in my day.

I need these things,
these talismans.
Otherwise my days
spin without catching
like a broken roulette wheel:
no risk,
but also no purpose.

Acknowledgments

I would like to thank the editors and publishers of the following reviews and magazines where these poems first appeared:

Etched Onyx: "My Super Power," "Obsession," "Escapes"
Santa Clara Review: "For Sara"
Red Booth Review: "Last Pennies"
Bare Root Review: "Seduction Confession"
Jellyfish Whispers: "The Three Bridges Trail"
Waldorf Literary Review: "Small Noise," "Our Drought," "Flurry of Wing and Talon," "Dusk at the Beach," "Cedar Swing"
New Plains Review: "Hands"
Lingerpost: "Prairie Storm"
Big River Poetry Review: "When Lilacs Bloom"
Garfield Lake Review: "Newspaper Days"
Pyrokinection: "The Lonely Stalk Their Front Room Windows At Night," "Wedding Photo," "Lavender," "What Holds You," "Voodoo Blue," "Freeze Out," "Fireball" "In The Beauty of All This," "Variations on Isolation"
Haunted Waters Press: "Twenty to Thirty Years"
The Dandelion Farm Review: "Once Was Home," "What a Good Walk Does"
Split Rock Review: "Pontoon Dream," "Night Light for the Harvest"
Pasque Petals: "Stars," "In With Dragonflies," "11:43," "A Shrine"
JMWW: "Crows Overhead," "Behind a Grove"
Perceptions: "Another Night"
Time of Singing: "The River Still"
South Dakota In Poems: "The Land Out Here"
Superpresent: "Bird on a Post"
The Fictional Cafe: "Rainbow," "Euthanized," "Teen-Age Days," "Hoops By Myself," "Refugees: To Go On Living"
Scurfpea: "Free-Fall"
Gatherings: "Sundays"
Petigru Review: "Blue Flannel"

Dana Yost was an award-winning daily newspaper journalist for 29 years. Since 2008, he has had nine books published, with *No Need to Walk in a Straight Line* his tenth. He is a three-time Pushcart Prize nominee, and a nominee for a Best of the Net poetry award.

Yost primarily worked at daily papers in Marshall, Minnesota, and Willmar, Minnesota. Among his major journalism awards, Yost twice was named the state's best daily newspaper columnist by the Minnesota Newspaper Association, won the best editorial portfolio award in an annual MNA contest, won first place for writing about politics in a contest by the Minnesota Associated Press Association contest, first place for feature writing from the South Dakota Press Association and was awarded the prestigious Journalism Accountability Award from the Minnesota Newspaper Council.

Among his notable books are the history book *1940: Journal of a Midwestern Town, Story of an Era* (Ellis Press), and the poetry books *Grace* (Spoon River Poetry Press) and *In Your Head* (South Dakota State Poetry Society). *In Your Head* won the annual SDSPS chapbook contest in 2020. He also won the 2015 Reader's Choice Award from *District Lit* for his poem "Where the Music Died."

Yost received a bachelor's degree in creative writing/literature from Southwest Minnesota State University. He served on the Minnesota Associated Press Association board of directors and serves on the South Dakota State Poetry Society board and was previously its president.
He lives in Sioux Falls, South Dakota.

www.ingramcontent.com/pod-product-compliance
Lightning Source LLC
Chambersburg PA
CBHW030057170426
43197CB00010B/1565